Ms. Sally's

Healthy Habit

Calendar Journal

for teens

and Teacher's Guide

Ms. Sally's

Healthy Habit

Calendar Journal

for teens

and Teacher's Guide

Sally Bradley

A Ms. Sally Book-www.Leemitt.com

Printed in the United States of America

Publishing services by Selah Publishing Group, LLC, Tennessee. The views expressed or implied in this work do not necessarily reflect those of Selah Publishing Group.

ISBN: 978-1-58930-266-2
Library of Congress Control Number: 2010914302

ATTITUDE

"The longer I live the more I realize the impact of attitude on life. It is more important than the past, than education, than money, than circumstances, than failures, than successes, than what other people think or say or do. It is more important than appearance, giftedness or skill. It will make or break a company... a church... a home.

The remarkable thing is we have a choice every day regarding the attitude we will embrace for that day. We cannot change our past... we cannot change the fact that people will act in a certain way. We cannot change the inevitable. The only thing we can do is play on the string we have, and that is our attitude... I am convinced that life is 10% what happens to me and 90% how I react to it.

And so it is with you... we are in charge of attitudes."

- Charles Swindoll

"**Motivation**

is what gets you started.

Habit is what keeps you going."

– Anonymous

January

The Positive Word Seed : Vision

vi·sion
Pronunciation: \ˈvi-zhən\
Function: *noun*
Etymology: Middle English, from Anglo-French, from Latin *vision-*, *visio*, from **vidēre** to see
Date: 14th century

1 a : something seen in a dream, trance, or ecstasy; *especially* : a supernatural appearance that conveys a revelation
b : a thought, concept, or object formed by the imagination
c : a manifestation to the senses of something immaterial <look, not at *visions*, but at realities — Edith Wharton>

2 a : the act or power of imagination
b (1) : mode of seeing or conceiving (2) : unusual discernment or foresight <a person of vision>
c : direct mystical awareness of the supernatural usually in visible form

3 a : the act or power of seeing : sight

4 a : something seen
b : a lovely or charming sight

— vi·sion·al *adjective*
— vi·sion·al·ly *adverb*

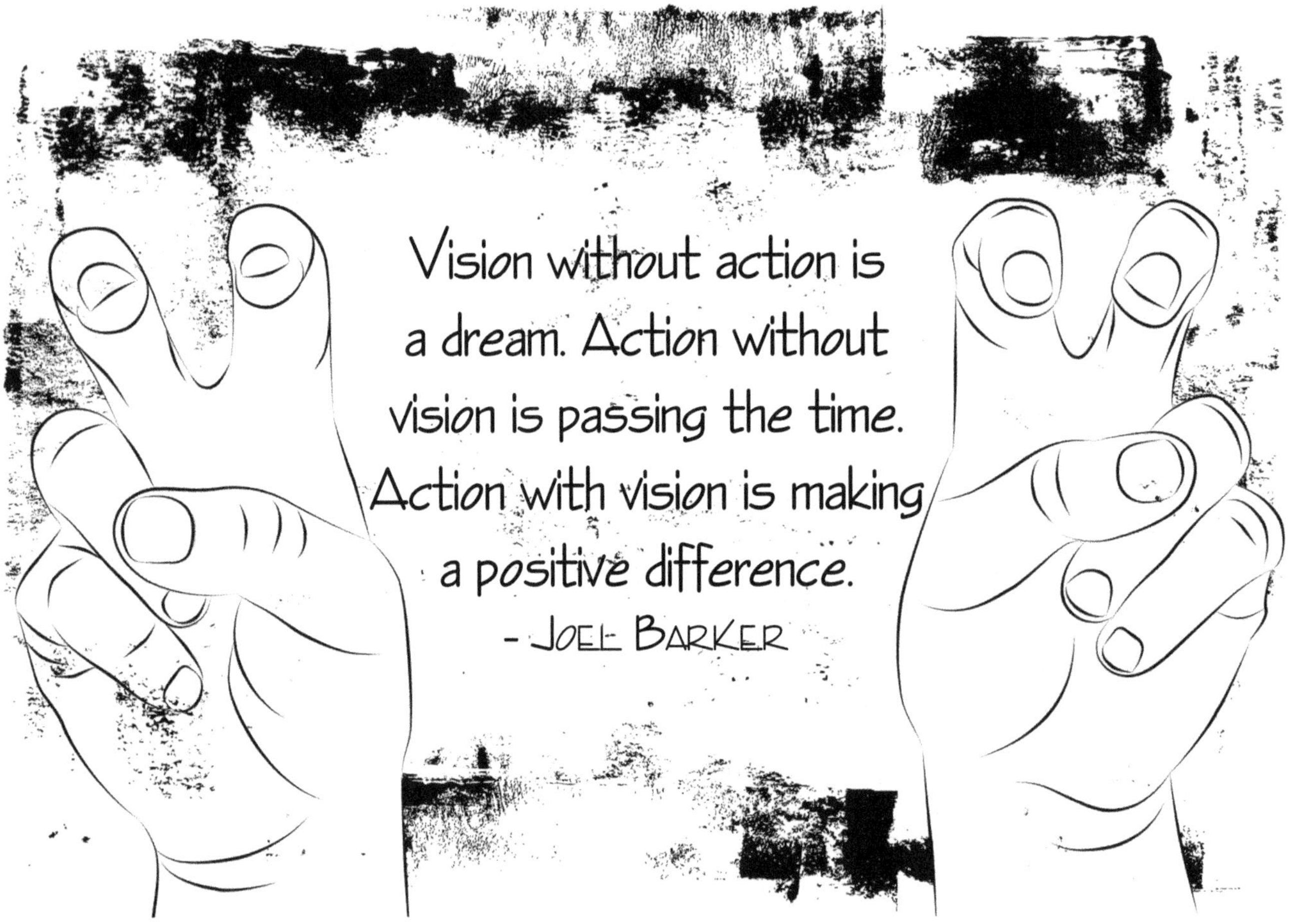
Vision without action is
a dream. Action without
vision is passing the time.
Action with vision is making
a positive difference.
- Joel Barker

JANUARY

Vision

Week 1

Action Steps

☐ Sunday

☐ Monday

☐ Tuesday

☐ Wednesday

☐ Thursday

☐ Friday

☐ Saturday

Vision

Positive Reinforcement

Sunday

Monday

Tuesday

Wednesday

Thursday

Friday

Saturday

JANUARY

Vision

Week 3

Role Playing

Sunday

Monday

Tuesday

Wednesday

Thursday

Friday

Saturday

JANUARY

Vision

week 4

Growing

Sunday

Monday

Tuesday

Wednesday

Thursday

Friday

Saturday

JANUARY

Notes

January Notes cont.

February

The Positive Word Seed : Goal Setting

Goal Setting: Purpose of any plan or action.

goal

Pronunciation: \'gōl

Function: *noun*

Etymology: Middle English *gol* boundary, limit

Date: 1531

2 : the end toward which effort is directed

— goal *intransitive verb*

— goal·less *adjective*

Goals are the fuel in the furnace of achievement.
- Brain Tracy

FEBRUARY

Goal Setting

Week 1

Action Steps

Sunday

Monday

Tuesday

Wednesday

Thursday

Friday

Saturday

Positive Reinforcement

Sunday ____________________

____

____

Monday ____________________

____

____

Tuesday ____________________

____

____

Wednesday ____________________

____

____

Thursday ____________________

____

____

Friday ____________________

____

____

Saturday ____________________

____

____

FEBRUARY

Goal Setting

Week 3

Role Playing

☐ Sunday ______________________________

____

____

☐ Monday ______________________________

____

____

☐ Tuesday ______________________________

____

____

☐ Wednesday ______________________________

____

____

☐ Thursday ______________________________

____

____

☐ Friday ______________________________

____

____

☐ Saturday ______________________________

____

____

FEBRUARY

Goal Setting

week 4

Growing

Sunday

Monday

Tuesday

Wednesday

Thursday

Friday

Saturday

FEBRUARY

Notes

March

The Positive Word Seed : Nutrition

nu·tri·tion

Pronunciation: \nu̇-ˈtri-shən, nyu̇-\

Function: *noun*

Etymology: Middle English *nutricioun*, from Late Latin *nutrition-, nutritio*, from Latin *nutrire*

Date: 15th century

1 : the act or process of nourishing or being nourished; *specifically* : the sum of the processes by which an animal or plant takes in and utilizes food substances

2 : nourishment

— nu·tri·tion·al \-ˈtrish-nəl, -ˈtri-shə-nəl\ *adjective*

— nu·tri·tion·al·ly *adverb*

Those who think they have
no time for healthy eating,
will sooner or later have to
find time for illness.
- Edward Stanley

Action Steps

Nutrition

☐ Sunday

☐ Monday

☐ Tuesday

☐ Wednesday

☐ Thursday

☐ Friday

☐ Saturday

MARCH

Nutrition

week 2

Positive Reinforcement

☐ Sunday ______________________________

____

____

☐ Monday ______________________________

____

____

☐ Tuesday ______________________________

____

____

☐ Wednesday ______________________________

____

____

☐ Thursday ______________________________

____

____

☐ Friday ______________________________

____

____

☐ Saturday ______________________________

____

____

MARCH

Nutrition

week 3

Role Playing

Sunday ______________________________

Monday ______________________________

Tuesday ______________________________

Wednesday ______________________________

Thursday ______________________________

Friday ______________________________

Saturday ______________________________

MARCH

Nutrition

week 4

Growing

☐ Sunday

☐ Monday

☐ Tuesday

☐ Wednesday

☐ Thursday

☐ Friday

☐ Saturday

MARCH

Notes

March Notes cont.

April

The Positive Word Seed : Communication

com·mu·ni·ca·tion

Pronunciation: \kə-ˌmyü-nə-ˈkā-shən\

Function: *noun*

Date: 14th century

1 : an act or instance of transmitting

2 a : information communicated

b : a verbal or written message

3 a : a process by which information is exchanged between individuals through a common system of symbols, signs, or behavior <the function of pheromones in insect communication>; *also* : exchange of information

b : personal rapport <a lack of communication between old and young persons>

4 *plural*

a : a system (as of telephones) for communicating

b : a system of routes for moving troops, supplies, and vehicles

c : personnel engaged in communicating

5 *plural but sing or plural in constr*

a : a technique for expressing ideas effectively (as in speech)

b : the technology of the transmission of information (as by print or telecommunication)

— com·mu·ni·ca·tion·al \-shnəl, -shə-nəl\ *adjective*

To wish you were someone else is to waste the person you are.
- Unknown

Communication

Action Steps

☐ Sunday ____________________

☐ Monday ____________________

☐ Tuesday ____________________

☐ Wednesday ____________________

☐ Thursday ____________________

☐ Friday ____________________

☐ Saturday ____________________

Communication

Positive Reinforcement

☐ Sunday ______________________________

____

____

☐ Monday ______________________________

____

____

☐ Tuesday ______________________________

____

____

☐ Wednesday ______________________________

____

____

☐ Thursday ______________________________

____

____

☐ Friday ______________________________

____

____

☐ Saturday ______________________________

____

____

APRIL

Communication

Week 3

Role Playing

Sunday

Monday

Tuesday

Wednesday

Thursday

Friday

Saturday

APRIL

Communication

week 4

Growing

Sunday

Monday

Tuesday

Wednesday

Thursday

Friday

Saturday

APRIL

Notes

April Notes cont.

May

The Positive Word Seed : Self-esteem

self-es·teem
Pronunciation: \-ə-ˈstēm\
Function: *noun*
Date: 1657

1 : a confidence and satisfaction in oneself : self-respect
2 : self-conceit

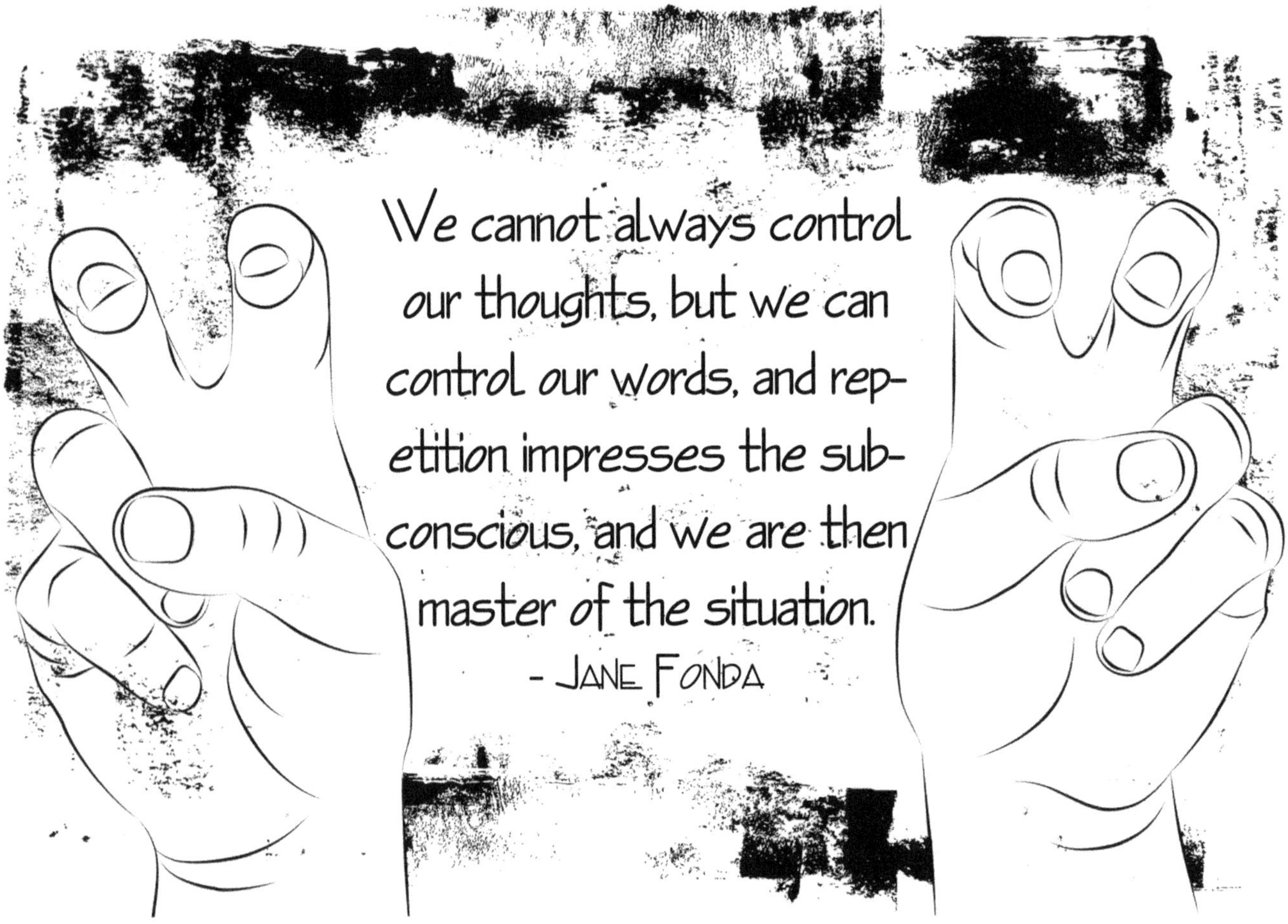
We cannot always control our thoughts, but we can control our words, and repetition impresses the subconscious, and we are then master of the situation.
- Jane Fonda

Self-esteem

Action Steps

☐ **Sunday** ____________________

☐ **Monday** ____________________

☐ **Tuesday** ____________________

☐ **Wednesday** ____________________

☐ **Thursday** ____________________

☐ **Friday** ____________________

☐ **Saturday** ____________________

Self-esteem

Positive Reinforcement

Sunday

Monday

Tuesday

Wednesday

Thursday

Friday

Saturday

Self-esteem

Role Playing

Sunday ______________________________

____

____

Monday ______________________________

____

____

Tuesday ______________________________

____

____

Wednesday ______________________________

____

____

Thursday ______________________________

____

____

Friday ______________________________

____

____

Saturday ______________________________

____

____

MAY

Self-esteem

Week 4

Growing

☐ Sunday

☐ Monday

☐ Tuesday

☐ Wednesday

☐ Thursday

☐ Friday

☐ Saturday

MAY

Notes

May Notes cont.

The Positive Word Seed : Attitude

at·ti·tude

Pronunciation: \ˈa-tə-ˌtüd, -ˌtyüd\
Function: *noun*
Etymology: French, from Italian *attitudine,* literally, aptitude, from Late Latin *aptitudin-, aptitudo* fitness
Date: 1668

1 : the arrangement of the parts of a body or figure : posture
2 : a position assumed for a specific purpose <a threatening attitude>
3 : a ballet position similar to the arabesque in which the raised leg is bent at the knee
4 a : a mental position with regard to a fact or state <a helpful attitude>
b : a feeling or emotion toward a fact or state
5 : the position of an aircraft or spacecraft determined by the relationship between its axes and a reference datum (as the horizon or a particular star)
6 : an organismic state of readiness to respond in a characteristic way to a stimulus (as an object, concept, or situation)
7 a : a negative or hostile state of mind
b : a cool, cocky, defiant, or arrogant manner

If you don't think
every day is a good day,
just try missing one.
- Cavett Robert

Attitude

Action Steps

- [ ] Sunday

- [ ] Monday

- [ ] Tuesday

- [ ] Wednesday

- [ ] Thursday

- [ ] Friday

- [ ] Saturday

Attitude

Positive Reinforcement

☐ Sunday ______________________________

____

____

☐ Monday ______________________________

____

____

☐ Tuesday ______________________________

____

____

☐ Wednesday ______________________________

____

____

☐ Thursday ______________________________

____

____

☐ Friday ______________________________

____

____

☐ Saturday ______________________________

____

____

Attitude

Role Playing

Sunday

Monday

Tuesday

Wednesday

Thursday

Friday

Saturday

JUNE

Attitude

week 4

Growing

Sunday

Monday

Tuesday

Wednesday

Thursday

Friday

Saturday

JUNE

Notes

July

The Positive Word Seed : Self-control

self-con·trol

Pronunciation: \-kən-ˈtrōl\

Function: *noun*

Etymology: Middle English *manere*, from Anglo-French, from Vulgar Latin **manuaria*, from Latin, feminine of *manuarius* of the hand, from *manus* hand — more at manual

Date: 1711

: restraint exercised over one's own impulses, emotions, or desires

— self–con·trolled *adjective*

The way we communicate
with others and with
ourselves ultimately
determines the quality
of our lives.
- Anthony Robbins

Self-control

Action Steps

☐ Sunday

☐ Monday

☐ Tuesday

☐ Wednesday

☐ Thursday

☐ Friday

☐ Saturday

Positive Reinforcement

☐ **Sunday** ______________________________

____

____

☐ **Monday** ______________________________

____

____

☐ **Tuesday** ______________________________

____

____

☐ **Wednesday** ______________________________

____

____

☐ **Thursday** ______________________________

____

____

☐ **Friday** ______________________________

____

____

☐ **Saturday** ______________________________

____

____

JULY

Self-control

week 3

Role Playing

Sunday ______________________________

Monday ______________________________

Tuesday ______________________________

Wednesday ______________________________

Thursday ______________________________

Friday ______________________________

Saturday ______________________________

Self-control

Growing

☐ **Sunday**

☐ **Monday**

☐ **Tuesday**

☐ **Wednesday**

☐ **Thursday**

☐ **Friday**

☐ **Saturday**

JULY

Notes

July Notes cont.

August

The Positive Word Seed : Character

char·ac·ter

Pronunciation: \ˈker-ik-tər, ˈka-rik-\
Function: *verb*
Inflected Form(s): shared; shar·ing
Etymology: Middle English caracter, from Latin character mark, distinctive quality, from Greek *charaktēr*, from *charassein* to scratch, engrave; perhaps akin to Lithuanian *žerti* to scratch
Date: 14th century

2 a : one of the attributes or features that make up and distinguish an individual
c : the complex of mental and ethical traits marking and often individualizing a person, group, or nation <the character of the American people>
d : main or essential nature especially as strongly marked and serving to distinguish <excess sewage gradually changed the character of the lake>

5 : reputation <the scandal has damaged his character and image>

6 : moral excellence and firmness <a man of sound character>

7 a : a person marked by notable or conspicuous traits <quite a character>

— char·ac·ter·less *adjective*

— in character : in accord with a person's usual qualities or traits <behaving in character>

— out of character : not in accord with a person's usual qualities or traits <his rudeness was completely out of character>

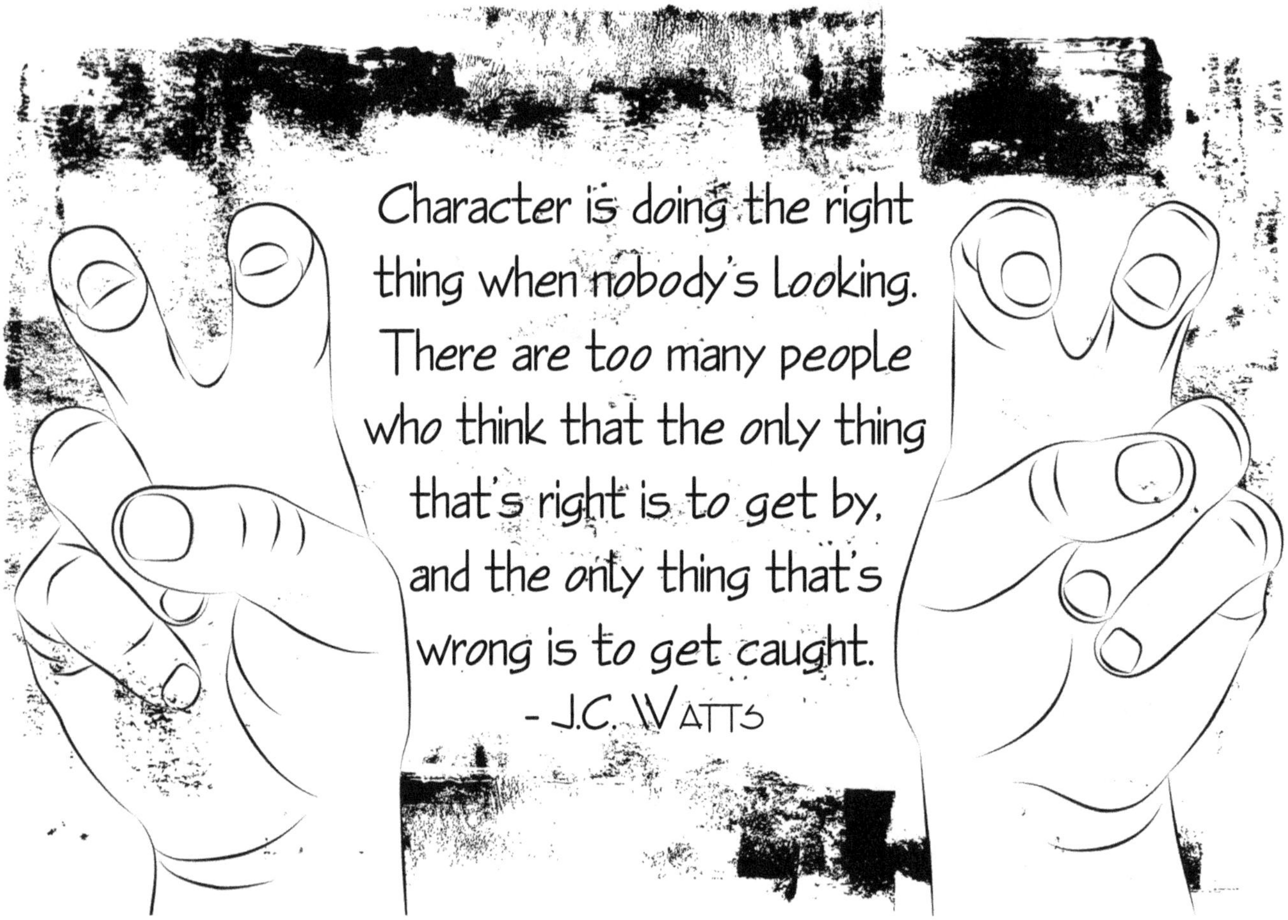
Character is doing the right thing when nobody's looking. There are too many people who think that the only thing that's right is to get by, and the only thing that's wrong is to get caught.
- J.C. Watts

AUGUST

Character

Week 1

Action Steps

☐ Sunday ______________________________

☐ Monday ______________________________

☐ Tuesday ______________________________

☐ Wednesday ______________________________

☐ Thursday ______________________________

☐ Friday ______________________________

☐ Saturday ______________________________

AUGUST

Character

Week 2

Positive Reinforcement

Sunday

Monday

Tuesday

Wednesday

Thursday

Friday

Saturday

AUGUST

Character

Week 3

Role Playing

☐ Sunday ________________________________

☐ Monday ________________________________

☐ Tuesday ________________________________

☐ Wednesday ________________________________

☐ Thursday ________________________________

☐ Friday ________________________________

☐ Saturday ________________________________

AUGUST

Character

Week 4

Growing

Sunday

Monday

Tuesday

Wednesday

Thursday

Friday

Saturday

AUGUST

Notes

September

The Positive Word Seed : Respect

re·spect
Pronunciation: \ri-'spekt\
Function: *noun*
Etymology: Middle English, from Latin *respectus*, literally, act of looking back, from *respicere* to look back, regard, from *re-* + *specere* to look — more at spy
Date: 14th century

1 : a relation or reference to a particular thing or situation <remarks having respect to an earlier plan>
2 : an act of giving particular attention : consideration
3 a : high or special regard : esteem
  b : the quality or state of being esteemed
  c *plural* : expressions of respect or deference <paid our respects>

Treat others as you want them to treat you because what goes around comes around.
- Unknown

Action Steps

☐ Sunday ______________________________

____

____

☐ Monday ______________________________

____

____

☐ Tuesday ______________________________

____

____

☐ Wednesday ______________________________

____

____

☐ Thursday ______________________________

____

____

☐ Friday ______________________________

____

____

☐ Saturday ______________________________

____

____

Positive Reinforcement

Sunday ______________________________

Monday ______________________________

Tuesday ______________________________

Wednesday ______________________________

Thursday ______________________________

Friday ______________________________

Saturday ______________________________

Role Playing

☐ Sunday ____________________

☐ Monday ____________________

☐ Tuesday ____________________

☐ Wednesday ____________________

☐ Thursday ____________________

☐ Friday ____________________

☐ Saturday ____________________

SEPTEMBER Respect

week 4

Growing

Sunday

Monday

Tuesday

Wednesday

Thursday

Friday

Saturday

SEPTEMBER

Notes

October

The Positive Word Seed : Think

think

Pronunciation: \'thiŋk\
Function: *verb*
Inflected Form(s): thought \'thȯt\; think·ing
Etymology: Middle English *thenken*, from Old English *thencan*; akin to Old High German *denken* to think, Latin **tongēre** to know — more at thanks
Date: before 12th century

transitive verb

1 : to form or have in the mind
2 : to have as an intention <*thought* to return early>
3 a : to have as an opinion <think it's so> b : to regard as : consider <think the rule unfair>
4 a : to reflect on : ponder <think the matter over> b : to determine by reflecting <think what to do next>
5 : to call to mind : remember <he never thinks to ask how we do>
6 : to devise by thinking —usually used with up <*thought* up a plan to escape>
7 : to have as an expectation : anticipate <we didn't think we'd have any trouble>
8 a : to center one's thoughts on <talks and thinks business> b : to form a mental picture of
9 : to subject to the processes of logical thought <think things out>

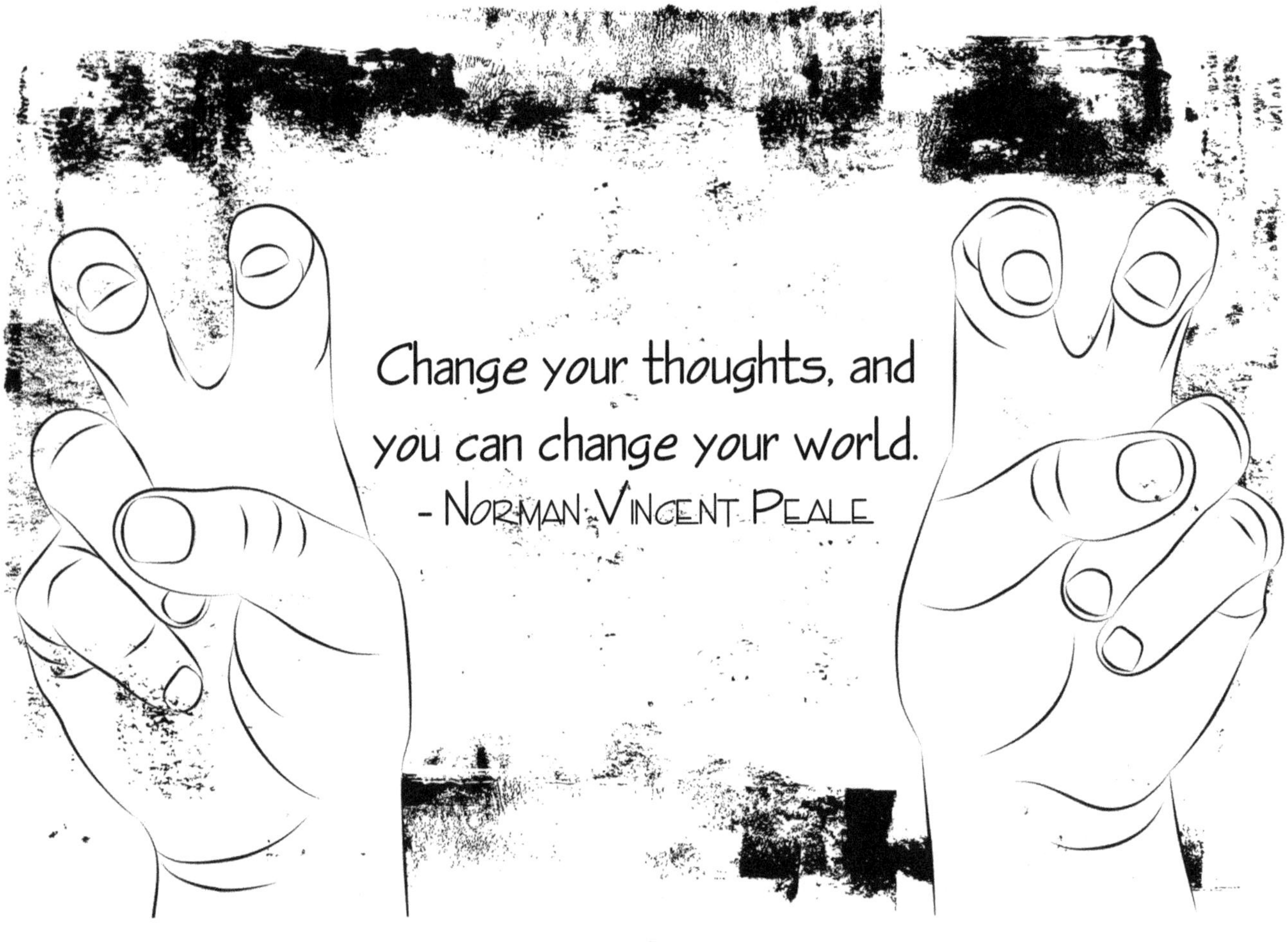
Change your thoughts, and
you can change your world.
- Norman Vincent Peale

Action Steps

Sunday

Monday

Tuesday

Wednesday

Thursday

Friday

Saturday

OCTOBER

Think

Week 2

Positive Reinforcement

☐ Sunday

☐ Monday

☐ Tuesday

☐ Wednesday

☐ Thursday

☐ Friday

☐ Saturday

OCTOBER

Think

Week 3

Role Playing

☐ Sunday

☐ Monday

☐ Tuesday

☐ Wednesday

☐ Thursday

☐ Friday

☐ Saturday

OCTOBER

Think

Week 4

Growing

☐ Sunday ______________________________

____

____

☐ Monday ______________________________

____

____

☐ Tuesday ______________________________

____

____

☐ Wednesday ______________________________

____

____

☐ Thursday ______________________________

____

____

☐ Friday ______________________________

____

____

☐ Saturday ______________________________

____

____

OCTOBER

Notes

November

The Positive Word Seed : Thankful

thank·ful

Pronunciation: \ˈthaŋk-fəl\

Function: *adjective*

Date: before 12th century

1 : conscious of benefit received <for what we are about to receive make us truly thankful>

2 : expressive of thanks <thankful service>

3 : well pleased : glad <was thankful that it didn't rain>

— thank·ful·ness *noun*

Be thankful for what you
have; you'll end up having
more, if you concentrate on
what you don't have, you will
never, ever have enough.
- Oprah Winfrey

NOVEMBER Thankful

Week 1

Action Steps

☐ Sunday ____

____

____

☐ Monday ____

____

____

☐ Tuesday ____

____

____

☐ Wednesday ____

____

____

☐ Thursday ____

____

____

☐ Friday ____

____

____

☐ Saturday ____

____

____

NOVEMBER

Thankful

Week 2

Positive Reinforcement

Sunday

Monday

Tuesday

Wednesday

Thursday

Friday

Saturday

NOVEMBER Thankful

Role Playing

☐ Sunday ______________________________

☐ Monday ______________________________

☐ Tuesday ______________________________

☐ Wednesday ______________________________

☐ Thursday ______________________________

☐ Friday ______________________________

☐ Saturday ______________________________

NOVEMBER **Thankful** week 4

Growing

Sunday

Monday

Tuesday

Wednesday

Thursday

Friday

Saturday

NOVEMBER

Notes

November Notes cont.

December

The Positive Word Seed : Prepare

pre·pare

Pronunciation: \pri-'per\
Function: *verb*
Etymology: Middle English, from Middle French *preparer*, from Latin *praeparare*, from *prae-* pre- + *parare* to procure, prepare
Date: 15th century

transitive verb

1 a : to make ready beforehand for some purpose, use, or activity <*prepare* food for dinner>
b : to put in a proper state of mind <is *prepared* to listen>

2 : to work out the details of : plan in advance <*preparing* a campaign strategy>

3 a : to put together : compound <*prepare* a prescription>
b : to put into written form <*prepare* a report>

intransitive verb

: to get ready <*preparing* for a career>

— pre·par·er *noun*

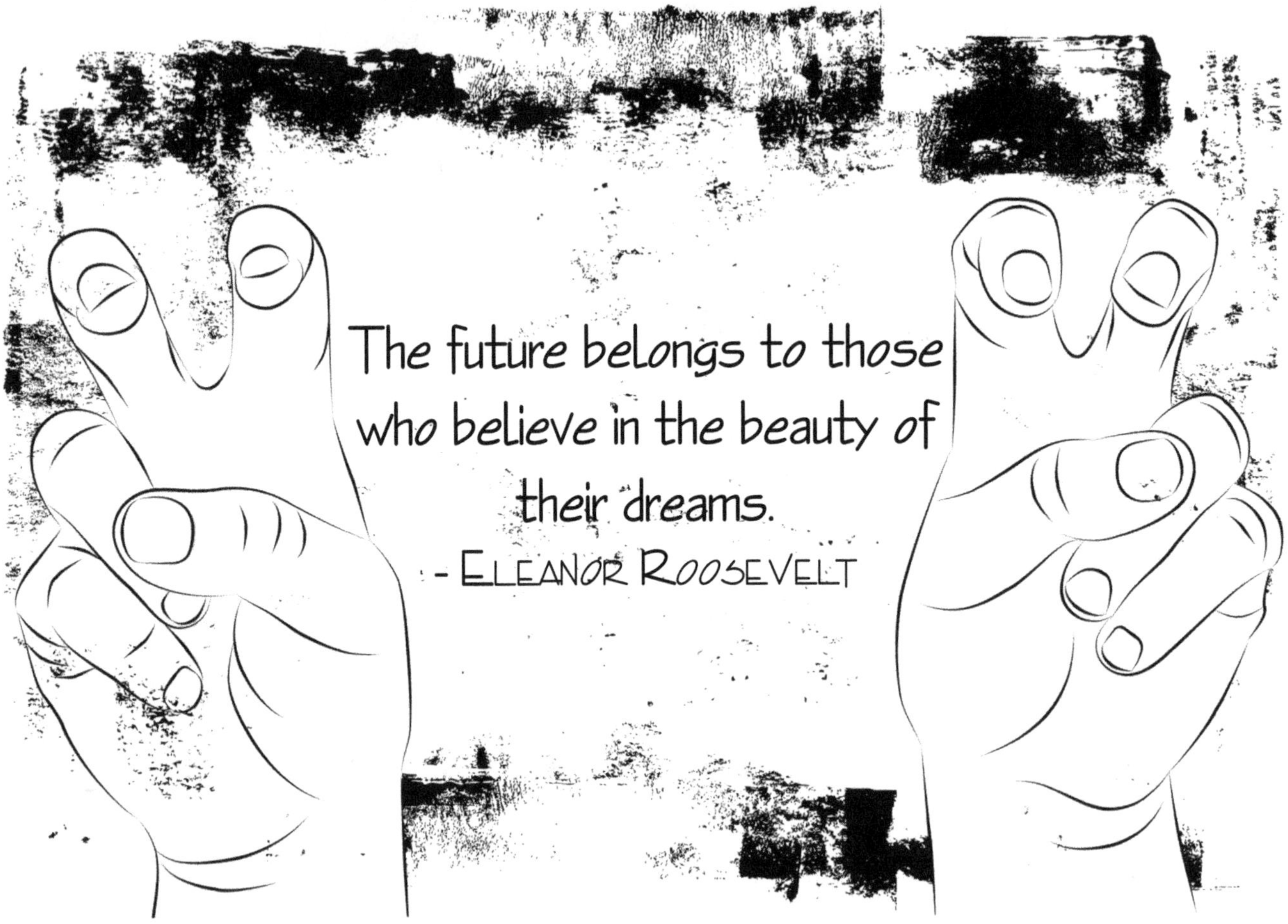
The future belongs to those
who believe in the beauty of
their dreams.
- Eleanor Roosevelt

DECEMBER

Prepare

Week 1

Action Steps

☐ Sunday ______________________________

____

____

☐ Monday ______________________________

____

____

☐ Tuesday ______________________________

____

____

☐ Wednesday ______________________________

____

____

☐ Thursday ______________________________

____

____

☐ Friday ______________________________

____

____

☐ Saturday ______________________________

____

____

DECEMBER Prepare

Week 2

Positive Reinforcement

Sunday

Monday

Tuesday

Wednesday

Thursday

Friday

Saturday

Prepare

Role Playing

☐ Sunday

☐ Monday

☐ Tuesday

☐ Wednesday

☐ Thursday

☐ Friday

☐ Saturday

DECEMBER

Prepare

week 4

Growing

Sunday

Monday

Tuesday

Wednesday

Thursday

Friday

Saturday

DECEMBER

Notes

To Teachers:

The major pursuit of "Ms. Sally's Healthy Habit Calendar Journals for teens is to help grow their minds with positive inputs to make better choices and goals for themselves.

This journal is also designed for interactive dialogue and open discussions.

INTRODUCTION

- More than 5 million children living today will die prematurely because of a decision they will make as adolescents---the decision to smoke cigarettes.
  Centers for Disease Control and Prevention

- Ten percent of all U.S. births are to teens
  Martin JA et al., Births: final data for 2002, National Vital Statistics Reports, 2003, Vol. 52, No. 10.

Ms. Sally's Healthy Habit Calendar Journal has been designed to reduce the dramatic increase in negative input that produces horrible effects in a youth's life both emotionally and physically.

This journal will:

- Target 8th thru 12 graders
- Promote positive self- image and healthy choices
- Build confidence, self esteem and proper behavior patterns
- Help teenagers learn to set goals and plan effectively
- Promote healthier eating habits
- Provide a good foundation for life skills
- Motivate and problem solve through role playing

Ms. Sally's Healthy Habit Calendar Journal is separated into four-week sessions, which include:

"POSITIVE WORD SEED". The students will be given the "POSITIVE WORD SEED" for the entire month. Students become what they program in their minds. With positive repetition students will have the ability to make better choices in life.

- **1st week:** "ACTION STEPS" section. In this section the teacher and the students will come up with some practical steps to incorporate the "POSITIVE WORD SEED" into their everyday lives at school, home, etc. This will help promote students to become more active in their writing, problem solving and planning skills.

- **2nd week:** "POSTIVE REINFORCEMENT" section. In this section the students will be able to reinforce the word of the month through encouraging one another by discussing the positive/negative consequences they may have for applying or not applying the "POSITIVE WORD SEED" of the month into their daily lives. This will build confidence, self-esteem, communication and healthy attitudes.

- **3rd week:** " ROLE-PLAYING" section. This is a fun way to motivate children to learn and problem solve. Teachers and students will come up with short skits for the "POSITIVE WORD SEED."

- **4th week:** " GROWING" section. In the last week for the "POSITIVE WORD SEED" of the month, the students will start growing from the inside, out, by remembering and using the "POSITIVE WORD SEED" in their everyday lives. This will help build a stronger foundation for a positive self-image, and proper behavior patterns.

Teacher Directed Mini Lessons

Each month you will have a POSITIVE WORD SEED that the students will be focusing on and developing through repetition.

For example: dealing with their Attitudes towards others, Patience, Communication, etc.

- In the first week, have the students state their plans in the "ACTION STEPS" section, listing specific daily actions that will help them become better people and students, demonstrating and using the "POSITIVE WORD SEED" of the month.

- In the second week, encourage the students in the "POSITIVE REINFORCEMENT" section of the planner by having them check one another's progress as well as their own. Have the entire class of students' names on pieces of paper, placed in a hat, have each student pull one name out of the hat, and have them encourage each other in pairs. Or, you can have an open discussion with the entire class. This is a great opportunity to talk on topics like: problem solving, respect, self-esteem, etc.

- In the third week, the "ROLE-PLAYING" section is a fun and simple way to motivate students. Have the students come up with short skits for the "POSITIVE WORD SEED" of the month. Have them act out the related word.

Example: The "POSITIVE WORD SEED" is Thankful. Have the students come up with a short skit using the word Thankful, such as when receiving, or having the opportunity to give someone a gift.

- In the fourth week, the "GROWING" section will be the last week of focus on the "POSITIVE WORD SEED" of the month. Have each student write in the "GROWING" section how the "POSITIVE WORD SEED" has made him or her more confident and how he or she will continue to use the "POSITIVE WORD SEED."

Positive Word Seed

January: __**Vision**__

This month will have the teenagers focus on there own personal dreams. Whether to become a doctor, lawyer, hairstylist, etc.

February: __**Goal Setting**__

This month will have the teenagers focus on setting positive goals to help reach there vision.

March: __**Nutrition**__

This month will focus on making healthy eating choices and exercise.

- March is National Nutrition Month.

April: __**Communication**__

Other words: talk, words, compliment, excuse me, shaking hands, smile.

May: __**Self-esteem**__

This month have the teenagers focus on there estimate of themselves and how vital it is to feel good about one's self.

June: __**Attitude**__

This month have the teenagers focus on how your attitude will determine the quality of life.

July: Self-control

This month have the teenagers focus on there own self control and how important it is to have.

August: Character

This is the month to have the teenagers focus on their character and the significance it has.

September: Respect

This is usually when teenagers return to school and they may have formed some bad habits during their vacation time. This is a great time to establish respect for others and themselves.

October: Think

This is the month to have them think before they react to situations.

November: Thankful

This is the month to focus on being thankful for each other.

December: Prepare

This is the month to have the teenagers prepare for the coming year.

To order additional copies of

Ms. Sally's

Healthy Habit Calendar Journal for teens

and Teacher's Guide

have your credit card ready and call
From USA: 1 800-917-BOOK (2665)
From Canada: (877) 855-6732

or e-mail
orders@selahbooks.com

or order online at
www.selahbooks.com

www.ingramcontent.com/pod-product-compliance
Lightning Source LLC
Chambersburg PA
CBHW062049090426
42740CB00016B/3065
* 9 7 8 1 5 8 9 3 0 2 6 6 2 *